Starting Right With
RABBITS

Netherland Dwarf male.
Photo by Michael Gilroy.

Starting Right With
RABBITS

by MERVIN F. ROBERTS

Title page:
Young rabbits, all under five months of age. At the top is a Red-eyed White, below is a Siamese Smoke and a Chinchilla (washing), beneath them is a Himalayan on the left and an Orange on the right, and at the bottom is an Agouti.

Photo credits: page 20 courtesy of the American Museum of Natural History; pages 23 (top), 46 (bottom) by M. Cummings; page 10 by M. Gilroy; page 24 by L. Goldman; title page and pages 19 (bottom), 38, 43 (bottom), 98 by R. Hanson; pages 31, 35, 50, 51, 59, 78, 79, 86, 87, 90, 91, 94, 95, 99, 102, 103 (top), 107 (top), 111 (bottom), 118, 119 by M. Roberts; pages 40, 42 (top), 47 (bottom), 48, 109 (bottom) by D. Robinson; pages 6, 11, 14, 15, 34, 39, 54, 55, 58, 62, 63, 66, 67, 70, 71, 74, 75, 82, 103 (bottom), 106, 107 (bottom), 110, 111 (top), 114, 115, 122, 123 by V. Serbin; page 80 by B. Taylor; page 42 (bottom) courtesy of the Texas Agricultural Service; page 112 courtesy of Three Lions, Inc.; page 117 courtesy of United States Department of Agriculture; page 109 (top) by C. Watkins.

t.f.h.

Distributed in the UNITED STATES by T.F.H. Publications, Inc., 211 West Sylvania Avenue, Neptune City, NJ 07753; in CANADA by Rolf C. Hagen Ltd., 3225 Sartelon Street, Montreal 382 Quebec; in ENGLAND by T.F.H. (Great Britain) Ltd., 11 Ormside Way, Holmethorpe Industrial Estate, Redhill, Surrey RH1 2PX; in AUSTRALIA AND THE SOUTH PACIFIC by Pet Imports Pty. Ltd., Box 149 Brookvale 2100 N.S.W., Australia; in SOUTH AFRICA by Multipet (Pty.) Ltd., 30 Turners Avenue, Durban 4001. Published by T.F.H. Publications Inc. Ltd., The British Crown Colony of Hong Kong.

Contents

Our thanks to the following people (and especially the delightful young people) who modeled for various of the photos in this book: KIM BIRCHALL, 59; SHANNON BIRCHALL, 50, 51, 102; A. BURKE, 79, 91; BRIAN JASIE, 35, 39; L. MC GUIRE, 90, 94; ALYCIA MASLOWSKI (*1981-82 ARBA Princess and winner of the Youth Royalty Contest*), 35, 39, 54, 62, 63, 70, 74; PETER MASLOWSKI, 11; CAROL MILLER, cover, 114; JENNIFER WINSHIP, 106, 107; KARIN WINSHIP, 58.

A champion Angora rabbit.

Introduction

It takes about four rabbit skins to provide the fur for one felt hat. It takes about one rabbit to find out if a woman is pregnant. It takes about one rabbit to provide a meal for four people. It takes a very knowledgeable person to determine whether a coat is genuine seal, squirrel, nutria, beaver, muskrat, leopard, ermine or just plain rabbit. It takes a patient and dedicated rabbit fancier to explain that a rabbit is a lagomorph and not a rodent. It takes a great number of words and pictures to describe all the different varieties of domesticated rabbit. As a matter of fact, there are more varieties of rabbits than of almost every other domesticated mammal—horses, cattle, cats, hamsters and guinea pigs included. Only domesticated dogs have more varieties.

The name "rabbit" seems to have originated in northern France. There is some evidence that this animal had a similar name in the language of the Flemish people four or five hundred years ago. In those good old days, and until the 18th century, an adult rabbit was frequently called a "coney" or "conie" or "cony" by English-speaking people, and only the juvenile was referred to as a rabbit. In fact, as recently as 1911, in English legal phraseology an adult rabbit was still a "cony." There is evidence that the Brooklyn, New York amusement park area called Coney Island was so named for the rabbits that were common there.

So now you may ask: if that is a rabbit, then what is a

hare? It is too bad that you asked. Let's go directly to square one and lay out the tree of life. Skip over the parts you already know and eventually the puzzle will be resolved.

THE TREE OF LIFE

Kingdom: Animalia. Life excluding protists, fungi and plants.

Phylum: Chordata. With a spinal cord. Here we part company with the arthropods, worms, mollusks, jellyfish, *etc., etc.*

Subphylum: Vertebrata. With a backbone. (There are a few chordates without backbones—the sea-squirt is one.)

Class: Mammalia. Nurse their young. Exit here the fishes, reptiles, amphibians, birds.

Subclass: Eutheria. With a placenta; this excludes the marsupials and the monotremes.

Order: Lagomorpha. Doubled incisors in the upper jaws.

Family: Leporidae. Excludes pikas.

A pika (sometimes spelled with a "c") looks like a big tailless gerbil until you examine those upper chisel teeth. There are four, as in all other lagomorphs. Not four in a row, but two in front and two more behind them. Hares and rabbits are set apart from pikas by their long hind legs, long ears, short cottony tails and soft fur. So, now with all the others out of the way, what is the *technical* difference between a hare and a rabbit?

The wild ancestor of our domestic rabbit was born blind, deaf and naked in an underground burrow. By contrast, a hare is precocious. That is, a hare is born with more fur, some vision, some hearing and a better ability to get about. It is born in a nest of grass called a "form" and not in a tunneled excavation underground.

Well, how about the Belgian Hare—isn't it born blind and naked? Yes, it is. Unfortunately, common popular names of animals often are misleading, and you just happened onto a good example of such a misnomer. The Belgian Hare is not a hare; it is just another variety of the domesticated rabbit.

The famous cheese and toast dish called a Welsh rabbit confuses the issue still further, and then the variant spelling Welsh "rarebit" compounds the confusion. Really, the name of this concoction was originally a joke; later, it seems, someone who didn't get the point of the original joke changed the name of the dish to rarebit.

Forget about these technicalities and simply call all rabbit-like long-eared *domesticated* animals rabbits. What about the burrowing wild rabbits of England? Yes, *they are* truly and properly *rabbits* and they *will mate* with our domesticated varieties. How about the American jackrabbit and cottontails? More about them later. What, then, is a bunny? Merely a cute name for any lagomorph, especially a young one at Eastertime.

A few paragraphs back, a limb of the tree of life was interrupted at the level of the family with a windy dissertation. Now here it would be appropriate to go the rest of the way out to the end of that limb of the tree.

Genus: *Oryctolagus*. Excludes the various genera of hares broken down to about thirty species and about a half dozen additional genera of rabbits encompassing perhaps two dozen species.

Species: *cuniculus*.

Oryctolagus cuniculus (Linnaeus) is the animal from which all of our domestic varieties have been developed through selective breeding. In some old books you may find references to *Lepus cuniculus*; this is an old name for our domesticated rabbit. Scientists subsequently changed *Lepus* to *Oryctolagus* to separate hares and some other rabbits from this genus of rabbits.

If you feel that even with all these facts you have been thrown into the briar patch, try looking at the

This full-grown dwarf albino fits easily into the author's hat.

Opposite:
Five-week-old Blue Silver Fox kittens
(above) and their mother (below).

domesticated rabbit another way. First, it has been propagated in captivity for perhaps 4000 years. Second, its wild ancestors were natives of the lands bordering the western Mediterranean Sea. Third, some varieties of this domesticated rabbit will survive and even thrive without our assistance in some parts of the world. Regardless of hair length or color or texture, regardless of body size or special features like ear size or dewlaps, all domesticated rabbits are as much the same species as all domesticated dogs are the same species and all domesticated hamsters are the same species.

The various jackrabbits of the central and western parts of the U.S. and Canada are all hares; their young are born suited with fur and with their eyes open. Although the cottontails of eastern North America are rabbits and their young are born blind, naked and helpless, they are not in the genus *Oryctolagus*. None of these wild American lagomorphs is related closely to the domesticated rabbit of European origin which we raise in cages. Don't waste your time or energy with jackrabbits or snowshoe hares or cottontails. None will breed readily in captivity. Most will not even survive in cages, and they will not interbreed with domesticated rabbits. Remember always that our domesticated caged rabbits are all one species, *O. cuniculus*, native to the lands of the western Mediterranean.

By nature, people tend to make rules and by *their* nature, animals manage to break the "rules." In this instance the distribution of the rabbit is the issue. Authorities must ignore the San Juan rabbit when they tell us that there are no established wild populations of *O. cuniculus* in the United States.

Off the coast of the state of Washington is the island of San Juan, and here the San Juan rabbit thrives. It does well there as a wild animal, and it also does well in captivity. It is about the size of a Dutch rabbit, and its color is usually brown with various shadings. This population has been established since about 1900 and is probably descended from Belgian Hares, with perhaps some Black Flemish and New Zealand ancestry as well. As happened with rabbits in Australia, someone released a few and they prospered. Be that as it may, it is unlikely that rabbits could take over on this continent as they did in Australia 100 years ago. Here competition, diseases, predators and parasites would surely keep their numbers down. Yes, there were also a few camels in the Wild Wild West once upon a time, but you need not worry about them either.

The scientific name *Oryctolagus* is from the Greek and translates to "burrowing hare." Many scientific names for animals are derived from Greek; this is especially true of generic names. The name is chosen by the person who first describes the organism in a published work. However, the specific name *cuniculus* is Latin and means "rabbit." It also means "a subterranean passage or cave" and suggests an animal which has its home underground.

The easiest way to classify mammals, especially when they superficially resemble each other, is by counting their teeth. A simple chart is laid out this way:

	Upper		Upper		Upper		Upper		
Incisors	-----	Canines	-----	Premolars	-----	Molars	-----	=	Total
	Lower		Lower		Lower		Lower		

Abbreviated, it looks so:

I-------   C-------   Pm-------   M----   = T.

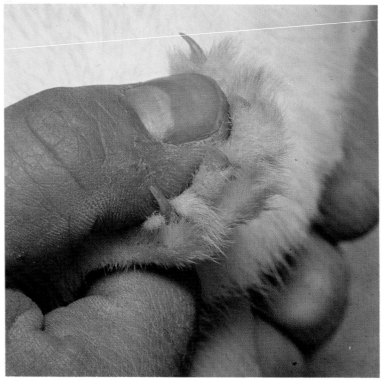

A "poor, defenseless" little rabbit has more to bargain with than you might think.

The numbers are for just one side (right or left) of both jaws, so the total is twice the tally of all the numbers shown.

For the rabbit, then:

$$\begin{array}{ccccc} 2 & 0 & 3 & 3 \\ I --- C --- Pm --- M --- = \text{Total } 28 \\ 1 & 0 & 2 & 3 \end{array}$$

$$(3 + 0 + 5 + 6) \text{ X } 2 = 28 \text{ teeth}$$

Lagomorph incisors (I) are the interesting teeth since the upper jaw has twice as many incisors as the lower. Also interesting is the fact that the second upper incisor is behind—not next to—the first. If you look at a rabbit head-on you won't see that tooth.

When zoologists think of introduced species, they automatically focus on rabbits in Australia and New Zealand. This is the classic case of an animal that was put where it had practically no enemies and where food was abundant and the climate was tolerable. We are told that seven domesticated rabbits were let loose in New Zealand near Invercargill about 1860; by another account, three pairs were released in New South Wales, Australia at about the same time. In still another account, a man named Thomas Austin had two dozen wild rabbits released on his land in Victoria. One thing is certain: they multiplied. This is an understatement. Their population exploded. Using conservative estimates for litter size, breeding age and frequency of litter production, it has been calculated that one pair could generate over thirteen million (13,000,000) additional rabbits in three years. No wonder there have been so many get-rich-quick schemes involving rabbits. Forget it. No one gets rich on rabbits.

In still another account, several hundred rabbits escaped from an Australian rabbitry in 1863 as the result of a fire. It is very likely that all of these various accounts are true or nearly so.

The rabbits that went wild in New Zealand and Australia were the same as the domestic species which we breed today. They are social, burrowing, born naked and very, very prolific. They eat grass and shrubs and leaves and fruit and even the bark of trees. There is no stopping them with dogs or snares or guns or poison.

Between 1936 and 1951 a viral disease called myxomatosis was developed to kill off some of these wild rabbits, and it certainly did kill rabbits. The disease is transmitted by the bite of mosquitoes or rabbit fleas acting as vectors. The scheme was nearly perfect except that there are many places in Australia where rabbits abound but where there isn't enough open, still shallow water to support a mosquito population to carry the disease from one rabbit to another. Another drawback developed. The disease spread to Great Britain and continental Europe, where rabbits are not a pest but are an important part of the food supply. In the British Isles, fleas are said to transmit the disease. Fortunately, myxomatosis is a disease which is lethal to only this one species of animal.

Recently the disease has become still less effective as a control, since the Australian rabbit is becoming increasingly resistant to the virus. Concerning the fleas, in case you wondered, they didn't survive the trip to Australia, and the native Australian flea just doesn't do the job.

To put this Australian rabbit business in perspective, during the peak years 1920 to 1935, the meat and skins

Himalayan rabbits have a distinctive color pattern.

Opposite:
The smooth and velvet-like fur of a Rex
rabbit (Smoke Pearl above) is much
shorter than the fur of a Polish rabbit
(Himalayan-marked below).

Although man can not contract myxomatosis from a rabbit, a wild rabbit may be a carrier of some disease transmissible to man and certainly may harbor parasites such as fleas and ticks —so avoid handling wild rabbits.

of Australian rabbits were exported for a reported value of more than $11,000,000, representing one hundred million rabbits. All this from a pest which caused more damage than it was worth.

If you should become interested in the behavior of wild *O. cuniculus*, the first book you should read is, surprisingly, a novel! This book, *Watership Down* by Richard Adams, was on the best seller lists for over a year and was number one for much of that time. It is available through booksellers and in most libraries.

Somewhat more technical and less fun to read is *The Private Life of the Rabbit*, by R.M. Lockley. This book is the definitive work on the wild version of the domesticated rabbit.

Rabbit Cousins

Within the family Leporidae, scientists have named and described about 30 species of hares and about 25 species of rabbits. Let's look briefly at the rabbits, genus by genus.

Oryctolagus - One species, *O. cuniculus*, native to lands of the western Mediterranean, was named *Lepus cuniculus* by Linnaeus in 1758. This species is precisely our domesticated rabbit; make no mistake about that. Introduced wild populations are now established in Australia, New Zealand, Chile, the British Isles, western continental Europe and a few isolated islands throughout the world. A half-dozen subspecies have been described; these subspecies vary in size and color and hair length, but all are readily recognizable as rabbits.

In addition, there are:

—four species from South Africa in the genus *Pronolagus*. Their tails are somewhat longer than those of *Oryctolagus*.

—one species from North India, Nepal and Assam, in the genus *Caprolagus*; it is somewhat darker in color than *Oryctolagus*.

—one Sumatran genus, *Nesolagus*, with one species.

—one Japanese genus, *Pentalagus*, with one species.

—fifteen New World species in the genus *Silvilagus*, including the familiar cottontail but not including the western U.S. jackrabbit, which is a hare.

—one genus from western North America,

An Arctic hare in its winter coat seems to blend into the snowy background.

Opposite:
A Belgian Hare (above) is really a rabbit while the brown hare (below) is a true hare.

23

You may be tempted to try to raise and care for a cute cottontail, but it won't survive for long in a cage.

Brachylagus, with but one species.

—one genus, *Romerolagus*, with one species from Mexico; it has small round ears and practically no tail. Nearly black, it looks more like a pika or a tailless rat than a rabbit.

—the genus *Lepus*, with over 25 species, is the big genus of true hares; it includes, among others, the Arctic hare and the familiar jackrabbit of western North America.

If you live in the eastern part of the United States and come upon cottontails, don't waste your time with them. They will not survive in cages for any length of time. Every spring someone gets his picture in the newspaper because his dog or cat has adopted one or two cottontail waifs, but by the following week the little fellows are invariably beset by some sad accident.

Rabbits in Legend and Literature

KITCKI MANITOU AND MICHABO

The religion of the Algonquin Indians of eastern North America is centered around the Great Spirit, Kitcki Manitou, dwelling in heaven and presiding over everything. Another spirit of lesser but still considerable importance is the Great Hare, Michabo. It is this Great Hare who created the earth, water and fish. Michabo also invented fishing nets and was the father of the Algonquin Indians. He lives where the sun rises, and he represents dawn. The Montagnais, a tribe of Algonquin Indians, believe that there was a flood (perhaps Noah's flood?) and that after the flood, Michabo re-established the earth.

Not only the American Indians but also the Chinese look up to the rabbit and hare. This reverence is tied into the Festival of the Moon, which takes place during the full moon of the autumn equinox. Children and women offer fruits to a little figure representing a rabbit.

Europeans have established a mythological role for the rabbit as the Easter Bunny, and somehow they managed to get it to deliver colored eggs. It would be hard to determine who—the eggshell dye industry or the rabbit breeders or the pet dealers or the poultry breeders—is behind all this, if anyone is. Inquiries always lead to blind alleys. Research in the literature provides several possibilities. One popular children's book tells us that

A rabbit playing his traditional role as the Easter Bunny.

Opposite:
A rock hyrax (above) and a tree hyrax (below). Although some people may think that there is at least a passing resemblance between a rabbit and a hyrax, the hyrax is actually more closely related to the elephant, partly because of its dental arrangement.

the rabbit somehow symbolized the moon in ancient Egypt; since the phases of the moon are used to establish the date for Easter, the book makes a connection between Easter and bunnies. That's one version.

In another tradition, a Teutonic goddess is credited with creating the Easter Bunny. She started with a bird that she changed into a rabbit. The rabbit, out of appreciation for its wonderful new form, laid colored eggs to help the goddess celebrate her annual spring festival. Of all the Easter Bunny stories, this one seems the most reasonable.

In still another account, which also sounds reasonable, rabbits (and chickens too) were venerated or admired because they are especially fertile in springtime. Some pre-Christian celebrations with these animals got carried over into our culture when the European pagans were converted.

There are four places in which the rabbit is mentioned in some translations of the Bible. In the Moffatt translation, we read in Leviticus 11:5,6 ". . . the hyrax because, although it chews the cud, it has not a parted hoof and therefore is unclean for you; the hare, because, although she chews the cud, she has not a parted hoof and therefore is unclean for you."

From Deuteronomy 14:7 we read ". . . you must not eat the following: the camel, the hare, and the hyrax, which are unclean for you since they chew the cud but have no divided hoof, also the pig. . ." If you read these passages in the King James version you will find "coney" instead of "hyrax."

If you are not familiar with a hyrax, suffice it to say that it is not a rodent such as the rat nor is it a lagomorph such as the rabbit. It is a member of the order Hyracoidea, more closely related to the rhinoceros and the elephant than to the rabbit.

What Rabbits Eat

Experienced rabbit breeders don't all agree, but then neither do all Republicans or all Irishmen or all members of the United Nations. Let us begin with one proven basic diet; later you can supplement it, if and when you see fit. The first essential component of the diet is water. It should be at least as clean, fresh and cool as what you enjoy drinking. If you cannot provide this, you have no business keeping rabbits, be it one or a thousand. Assume that each four-pound rabbit requires a pint a day to drink and (unless your delivery system is absolutely perfect) another pint to waste. Bear in mind that a doe nursing babies must also drink for all of them as well. Remember that ice is no substitute for water. Your rabbits should ideally have clean fresh water before them at all times.

The second element of rabbit diet is, of course, food. Contrary to what many people believe, food for rabbits doesn't mean just carrots and lettuce. Carrots and lettuce are hardly more than inconsequential supplements.

It is so simple to feed a rabbit properly that most people don't quite believe it. All a rabbit needs in addition to the drinking water is a high-quality dust-free, fresh, clean, dry, high-protein pelletized rabbit food, available just that way in pet shops and farm supply stores. The better rabbit pellets were developed by professional animal nutritionists to provide all the calories, vitamins, minerals, roughage, proteins, *et cetera* required from

The most immediately obvious and distinctive feature of this English Lop rabbit is the length of the ears. Photo by Ray Hanson.

Opposite:
Carrots and other vegetables should be used only to supplement a rabbit's basic diet of pelletized rabbit food.

cradle to grave. Pellets vary in their ingredients from brand to brand, but most are based on alfalfa, cereal grains, salt and other mineral additives and even some animal matter, such as bone meal.

Bear in mind that hamster pellets are intended for hamsters and that rabbit pellets are intended for rabbits. Provide the pelletized food that was specifically made for rabbits; it is so easy to do it right.

One reason why rabbit diet is not the same as hamster or gerbil or guinea pig diet is that the digestive system of the rabbit is not like that of those other animals. A mouse, for example, chews and swallows and digests; it then eventually excretes feces and urine. A cow chews and swallows and regurgitates and re-swallows its food (chews its cud), which is thus more fully digested, and eventually excreted.

A rabbit does it in a still different way. Food is quickly chewed and swallowed. Then, after it passes through the alimentary canal, it is finally excreted from the anus, and certain soft pellets are swallowed again to complete the digestive process. In this manner, the rabbit is able to eat rapidly and then thoroughly digest its food in the security of its burrow. The soft pellet is excreted and re-ingested while the wild rabbit is in its burrow, but the fully digested hard pellet, which is not of any further use to the rabbit, is always evacuated away from where the animal sleeps. Wild buck rabbits are believed to so mark the limits of their territories.

Many people who have kept rabbits for years have never observed this process; it is often performed early in the morning and so quickly that it passes unnoticed. Technically this re-ingestion is properly called coprophagy; rest assured that it is perfectly normal for a rabbit.

That fully digested fecal pellet which is of no value to the rabbit is great for raising earthworms, and it is also great for improving the quality of soil in the garden. A large rabbit might produce as much as two hundred pounds of manure per year, much desired by both gardeners and farmers. For more about this, you should read David Robinson, *The Encyclopedia of Pet Rabbits*, TFH Publications, Neptune, New Jersey, 1979.

Now that you know how simple it is, you may if you wish develop specialized diets for special conditions. The basic requirements as spelled out in the U.S. Dept. of Agriculture Handbook No. 309 are as follows:

	For dry does, herd bucks and developing young %	*For pregnant does and does with litters of nursing young* %
Crude Protein:	12 to 15	16 to 20
Fat:	2 to 3.5	3 to 5.5
Fiber:	20 to 27	15 to 20
Nitrogen-free extract:	43 to 47	44 to 50
Ash:	5 to 6.5	4.5 to 6.5

If the pelletized food is made by a reputable firm and kept vermin-free and dry and cool until it is fed, the necessary vitamins will all be present in their correct proportions.

A five-pound rabbit will eat four or five ounces of dry pellets per day if hay or straw for bedding is also available to supplement the diet. The weight of the hay

A Dutch-marked doe and her litter nibble from a dish of pellets. They *need* no other solid food.

Opposite:
A Netherland Dwarf with some of the drugs and diet supplements available for rabbits.

cannot be conveniently measured, since much of it goes out as soiled bedding, but it could easily amount to at least half a pound per day.

Rabbits will eat grass, cabbage, lettuce, carrots, potatoes, rutabaga, Jerusalem artichokes and apples. The list goes on and on. A few plants (such as western milkweed) are poisonous, but if you stick to conventional forage vegetation and things you thrive on, they will prove wholesome for your rabbits also.

To get started right, you should restrict the variety and stick to an unlimited supply of:

1.) high-protein rabbit pellets

2.) clean, dry, dust-free timothy hay or oat straw for both roughage and bedding

3.) all the fresh water they could possibly want, always available

4.) for an occasional treat or diet supplement, you could furnish the fresh vegetables previously mentioned.

Most rabbits will not eat a tomato or a banana or citrus fruits.

Baby rabbits and nursing (lactating) does could be helped tremendously with fresh milk soaked up by stale bread. (Not moldy bread, but simply dried bread.) Remember, these substances are supplements; they do *not* replace the basic pellet and water ration.

The reason why food and water should be always available is that when a rabbit is awake it is almost always eating. Rabbits are continuous eaters when they are at ease.

A salt block to lick is perhaps good insurance, but it is not necessary if the pelletized rabbit ration was properly prepared. Buy pellets from a reliable source. Do not swap brands if you know that your animals are thriving on what they are getting. Rabbits do best on an unvarying routine.

When a doe eats her young, it could have been because

she was frightened or molested or crowded. It could also have been because she was inadequately nourished. If a young doe eats her first litter, try to find out what went wrong and correct the problem. Then let her rest alone in a cage a month or two before breeding her again. If she cannibalizes her young a second time—and other does in your rabbitry are raising their babies—never breed her again; better still, get rid of her. Don't let sentiment cause you to lower the quality of your breeding stock.

It might be mentioned in passing that the vitamins will take care of themselves if all other aspects of rabbit nutrition are correct. For example, there seems to be no need for vitamin C additives, since rabbits produce this vitamin themselves. Vitamin D is probably necessary, and small amounts are present in the pellet ration. It is interesting to know that an excess of vitamin D may actually be injurious.

Vitamin E is present in cereal grains, so it too will be found in the pellet ration you provide.

Vitamin B is created by bacteria that live in the intestines of every rabbit. When rabbits re-ingest their soft droppings, they get the necessary vitamin B. This vitamin is also present in cereal grains.

Vitamin A is readily available in many green plants. It is probably unnecessary to add any to the diet so long as the pellets come from a reliable source.

After consideration of what goes into a rabbit, it is worthwhile to dwell for a moment on what comes out. Urine and hard droppings are excreted daily outside the sleeping area. If you give your animals sufficient room and a wise arrangement of nest, food and water, you will find that the droppings are usually deposited in just one place. If the screen openings in the cage floor are the right size, you will discover that it is easy to keep the cage clean. The odors, flies and vermin frequently associated with many caged animals are not difficult to

Food and water bowls should not be able to be tipped over. Here a guinea pig and a rabbit sip water from a sturdy bowl.

Opposite:
A white Angora and an assortment of feed and water accessories. Remember that your pet can easily knock down another rabbit and will probably practice on any cage furniture available.

Your rabbits should always have clean fresh water available, and an easy way to provide it is by attaching a gravity-feed water bottle to the outside of each rabbit's hutch.

eliminate, and an added dividend from rabbits is the manure.

Rabbit manure is a highly desirable material that can be used in gardens and around shrubs, trees and flowers. It will not "burn" plants. It is high in nitrogen. It is safe on crops. It is great for raising earthworms. If the rabbit droppings fall into boxes containing earthworms, you will be in the earthworm business, and the casts produced by the worms are excellent for improving the quality of any garden or potting soil. Worms in rabbit manure will eliminate the possibility of objectionable odors and will also reduce the number of flies in warm weather.

Choosing A Pet Rabbit

PUREBRED OR MONGREL?

Do you want a pet? A mongrel is as good as a registered purebred rabbit if all you want is one pet rabbit.

Do you want rabbit hair products? An Angora rabbit will provide enough for several pairs of gloves every year and still be a good pet.

Do you want rabbits you can eat? All rabbits are edible. Their meat is much like chicken, but it is all white meat and generally higher in protein and lower in fat than most poultry. Some varieties grow faster on less food, so these meat producers are what you should look for. New Zealands are outstanding for production.

Do you want rabbits you can show in competition? There are more than 50 varieties to choose from. They range in weight from two pounds to twenty and from shorthaired satin and rex types to the longhaired Angora. Their colors and patterns would take a book to describe. Some have dewlaps; some don't. You can join a specialty club and keep busy for the rest of your life breeding and exhibiting rabbits. You will add new dimensions to your life as you meet interesting people and strive to maintain and improve your animals.

RABBIT BREEDS

There can be no complete permanent list of rabbit breeds; so long as we have genetic variation and selective

Four popular breeds of rabbits: English Spot (opposite, above), Champagne d'Argent (opposite, below), Californian (right) and Chinchilla (below).

breeding, the list will never end. Some varieties may cease to be popular and may even disappear, but at the same time rabbit breeders will find new mutations and from them will establish new breeds. In 1971, the American Rabbit Breeders Association (ARBA) listed standards for more than 25 breeds, broken down further into over 75 varieties. If you are interested in these standards, you should join the ARBA and obtain the latest version directly from them. The Agricultural Research Service of the U.S. Department of Agriculture (in Handbook No. 309, titled *Commercial Rabbit Raising*) tabulated the features of thirteen popular breeds, and information from this table is reproduced here for your convenience.

American Chinchilla: COLOR: Resembles the true chinchilla, *Chinchilla laniger*. WEIGHT: 9-12 pounds. PRINCIPAL USES: Show and fur.

Californian: COLOR: White body; colored nose, ears, feet and tail. WEIGHT: 8-10½ pounds. PRINCIPAL USES: Show and meat.

Champagne d'Argent: COLOR: Undercolor a dark slate blue; surface color a blue-white or silver with a liberal sprinkling of long black guard hairs. WEIGHT: 9-12 pounds. PRINCIPAL USES: Show and meat.

Checkered Giant: COLOR: White with black spots on cheek, sides of body and on hindquarters; wide spine stripe; black ears and nose with black circles around the eye. WEIGHT: 11 pounds or over. PRINCIPAL USES: Show and fur.

Dutch: COLOR: Black, blue, chocolate, tortoise, steel-gray and gray; white saddle, or band, over the shoulder carrying down under the neck and over the front legs and hind feet. WEIGHT: 3½-5½ pounds. PRINCIPAL USES: Show and laboratory.

English Spot: COLOR: Basic body color white; colors of spots: black, blue, chocolate, tortoise, steel-gray, lilac and gray; nose, ear , and eye circles and cheek spots; spine stripe from base of ears to end of tail; side spots from base of ears to middle of hindquarters. WEIGHT: 5-8 pounds. PRINCIPAL USES: Show, meat and laboratory.

Flemish Giant: COLOR: Steel-gray, light-gray, sandy, black, blue, white and fawn. No two colors allowed on solids. WEIGHT: 13 pounds or over. PRINCIPAL USES: Show and meat.

Himalayan: COLOR: Same as Californian. WEIGHT: 2½-5 pounds. PRINCIPAL USES: Show and meat.

New Zealand: COLOR: White, red or black. WEIGHT: 9-12 pounds. PRINCIPAL USES: Show, meat and laboratory.

Polish: COLOR: White, black or chocolate; ruby-red eyes or blue eyes. WEIGHT: 3½ pounds. PRINCIPAL USES: Show and laboratory.

Rex: COLOR: Representative of any breed. WEIGHT: 7 pounds or over. PRINCIPAL USES: Show and fur.

Satins: COLOR: Black, blue, Havana brown, red, chinchilla, copper, Californian and white. WEIGHT: 8-11 pounds. PRINCIPAL USES: Show and fur.

Silver Martens: COLOR: Black, blue, chocolate or sable, with silver-tipped guard hairs. WEIGHT: 6½-9½ pounds. PRINCIPAL USES: Show and fur.

One reason why white rabbits are especially desirable for fur is that white rabbit fur can be dyed virtually any color. Most colored rabbit furs started out as white pelts. Unfortunately, rabbit fur is not as durable as otter, mink, sable, marten, muskrat or nutria. A Californian rabbit is still considered a white rabbit, since the dark extremities of the pelt are always removed anyway.

Four more popular rabbits: Flemish Giant (opposite, above), New Zealand White (opposite, below), young albino (right) and Siamese Sable Satin (below).

A view along one side of a rabbitry in which the hutches are made of wood. Many breeders prefer all-steel cages so that they don't have to worry about damage from the rabbits' gnawing and chewing.

Housing

A rabbit *cage* is generally considered to be a simple six-sided enclosure of metal mesh with some reinforcement at the corners. A *hutch* is generally regarded as a two-part enclosure consisting of a screened cage section attached to a weather-tight section. The screened section is where the animal finds its food and water and where it defecates and urinates. The enclosed portion is where it sleeps and where the doe bears and rears its young.

If you elect to keep your rabbit caged outdoors, the cage must be situated under a shed or a roof of some kind to provide protection from the elements, even including long periods of direct sunlight. Be sure that your pet can get out of sun, rain, cold winds and sub-freezing temperatures. It is one thing to have your rabbit hop around in its cage during a light summer's rain or a short snowfall. It is entirely another matter to deprive it of a place to dry off and warm itself. It must have a bone-dry place to sleep or it surely will sicken.

Use some judgment as you select the housing for your first animals. A small exhibition Rex cannot possibly do as well in the cold as a larger, tougher meat breed such as a New Zealand Red. Visit an experienced rabbit keeper in your vicinity; this person has already discovered how the local climate affects rabbits. In Florida you might do well with cages under a shed with cooling ventilation. In summertime the cooling problem could be your major consideration. In North Dakota or Maine, those cages

A hutch at eye-level (left) is good for the rabbit keeper because problems are easy to see and correct. It is also good for the rabbit because it provides some security from dogs and vermin. The floor screen (below) permits droppings to fall through, and the board is a resting place which helps prevent sore hocks. It is also warmer in winter, since the metal tends to carry away the animal's heat. A cloth cover (opposite, above) helps provide extra cold-weather protection for an outdoor hutch, and a screen covering on the inside of a wooden hutch (opposite, below) protects the wood from being chewed up.

51

would have to be indoors or hutches with canvas curtains and hay-filled nest boxes would be required. People have kept and bred rabbits just about everywhere, but the housing made up for the differences in climate. A sidelight on climate control is found in the does' habit of lining nests with belly fur. You will find that the insulating value of their fur is tremendous, and so long as the hutch is tight, the babies will be warm.

Start out small and walk before you run. A junior buck, an unrelated senior buck, a bred senior doe and a junior doe is the largest herd you should begin with. Better still, just for starters, just one unrelated buck, a junior doe and a bred senior doe. In this way you will have several bloodlines to work with and just a few animals to house while you are learning the ropes. In a few weeks that senior doe will have kindled and you will be elated!

Start out with a few animals and a cage or a hutch for each and a spare one for what comes naturally. Of course, if you are especially cautious or your funds are limited, you could begin with one large cage or hutch and just one bred senior doe.

Don't build an orange-crate hutch if you are serious about starting right with rabbits. They deserve better than that. Nowadays, wooden hutches or wood-frame cages are the second choice of experienced rabbit keepers. Rabbits do chew or gnaw or otherwise destroy wood. They do it out of boredom or to escape or to visit friends or because the wood tastes better than what they are being fed. Perhaps they crave more salt. An all-steel cage will last longer, ultimately cost less, can be sterilized easily, will not get smelly and will not be chewed to bits.

Buy at least your first cage or hutch from your pet dealer or through the advertising in your rabbit club magazine. Then after you have had some personal experience with it, you may elect to buy more of the same or you might decide to build your own. It is not difficult, but it will cost something to do it right. You will find that the individual rabbit is the smallest part of your investment.

A wire mesh bottom to the cage or the screened part of the hutch is a great way of keeping the cage or hutch free of the droppings and urine. Just provide a large tray or box under this mesh floor and you can raise earthworms.

If you have a source of supply for wine barrels or steel drums or heavy shipping crates or nail kegs, you might be able to adapt these containers for use as hutch enclosures or nest boxes. Various money-saving schemes for housing rabbits have been tried over the past several thousand years. Some are really ingenious.

The Romans carried rabbits to the lands they conquered to provide fresh meat and there they enclosed them with stone fences. The wild rabbits of the British Isles probably came with the Romans, but their domestic descendants (same species) were likely brought from France with the Normans five hundred or so years later.

Getting back to the hutch and cage arrangements, you should bear in mind that eight rabbits might consume as much as a gallon of water a day—that is a pint per rabbit per day if they are fed dry food only. You could end up doing a lot of walking with water if you want to keep a number of animals any distance from a spigot. Remember that rabbits must drink (they don't normally eat snow or gnaw ice) at least once every day and preferably on demand. If you keep a few pets in your home or in a nearby garage, there is no water problem, but if you think bigger and live in an area where winter brings a hard frost, you must carefully work out the water supply before spending any money on cages.

The delivery of food is hardly a problem if you plan to base the diet on pellets and supplement it with hay, green foods and perhaps stale bread. All sorts of self-feeder hoppers are available from pet dealers and farm

This Dwarf rests in a bed of soft bright hay. This bedding material will give the animal a feeling of security, will protect it from drafts, will absorb any spills which might otherwise soil its coat—and might even be nibbled.

Opposite:
Alycia wears a popular style white coat when she works with rabbits. It is washable and sturdy. The pockets are handy for nail clippers, grooming aids, and perhaps even a small carrot. The cage is a popular design and is more than adequate to transport two small rabbits.

supply stores. Mount the hopper where it will not get wet. Dry pellets are great rabbit food, but wet or damp pellets will disintegrate and ferment or get moldy. The effect of fermentation or mold on the rabbit is about the same. He will surely sicken and he may die. It is a waste of effort to list the diseases caused by bad food. Knowing their names will get you nowhere. The best control for most diseases of domestic rabbits is not medicine; it is hygiene. Give them clean, dry, well-ventilated, uncrowded quarters, wholesome food and the same water you enjoy drinking; they will likely go for generations with no serious disease.

Another aspect of getting rabbit food to the rabbits is that rats and mice also will thrive on the same stuff. Not only will they steal the food, but they will also contaminate it with their feces and urine. Also, some diseases are common to these rodents and to rabbits, so another problem for you is to keep these vermin out of your rabbitry. Rats will also kill and eat newborn rabbits if they can get to them. So, you may choose to keep a few cats. Well, maybe and maybe not—cats, like mice and rats, can carry diseases and parasitic worms to your caged animals. It may look "farmer-cute" to have a cat curled up on the top of a bag of oats or pellets, but that is not the way to keep your rabbits in the best of health. The cat may be able to cope with its tapeworm, but for the rabbit, this might just be the last straw.

Store pellets, grain and even hay in clean metal or plastic garbage cans with tight-fitting lids. Sweep up spills. Trap rodents; don't rely solely on a cat.

Remember, too, that mice, rats, cats and dogs may molest your rabbits to the point where does will resorb their unborn young or kill or desert their litters. This cautionary note also goes for playful young children. Supervise your visitors and enjoy your experience with rabbits.

Handling Rabbits

Sadly, a great number of young rabbits are mishandled and even killed every Easter—so much so that in some places there are legal restraints on the sale of "Easter Bunnies". Some abuse is just plain cruelty by people who are just naturally cruel, but mostly the problems stem from ignorance. Children who never had a pet suddenly have a young animal (which resembles a doll) thrust upon them. There is no instruction and no understanding and soon there is no rabbit.

If you plan to give a rabbit to a child, remember that getting the animal itself is the easiest part of the transaction. All you need is money. The rest is much more difficult and also much more rewarding. Prepare for the pet with adequate housing. A corrugated cardboard box is not a proper rabbit cage. A dog or a cat can easily get in and kill the rabbit or worry it to death. The bottom has no provision for urine and droppings. Ventilation in a carton is never right. A good cage will probably cost as much or even more than the rabbit did, but it is vital to the life and well-being of the animal.

A tame rabbit enjoys gentle human company. It will respond to loving care. It won't purr like a cat or whine like a dog, but it will sit in your lap and enjoy being stroked. Although rabbits are not high on any list of house pets and most are kept in garages, sheds, hutches and cages, it is possible to keep a rabbit in the home. Some have even been paper trained.

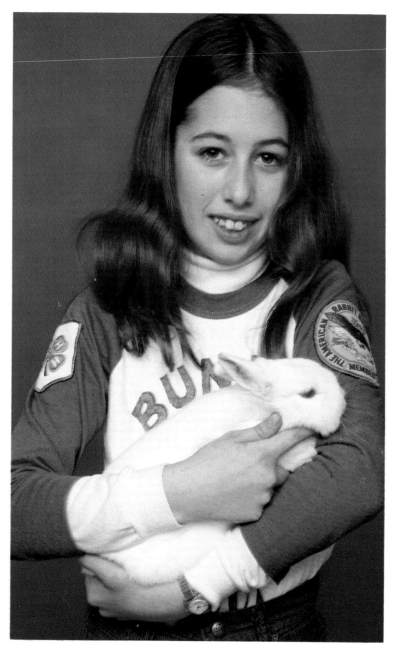

Notice the 4-H Club insignia on this girl's right shoulder. Also notice how she cradles the animal without squeezing it.

If you cradle a rabbit so that it feels secure but not squeezed you are less liable to get scratched.

So, if you give (or get) a pet rabbit, be sure it is accompanied by some instructions. The first instruction is a rule. *Don't ever lift a rabbit by its ears!* Rabbit ears are delicate and easily injured. Pick up a rabbit by firmly grasping the loose skin across its shoulders and support its rump from below with your other hand. The rabbit is carried with its head high and its tail low. That is to say, belly up. One reason for this is to protect you from those powerful hind legs and their sharp toenails. Of course if you have one or two tame pets, you will soon find that they can be cradled in your arms in perfect safety.

Any rabbit can bite and some do. If you don't know the animal, don't take chances with it.

Another thing about handling rabbits is that some have fleas. They need not, but some do. These fleas are a pest. Also they may transmit diseases from one animal to another. Also you may be the transmitter of fleas from one rabbit to another—or from your pet dog or cat to a rabbit. Dog fleas and rabbit fleas are not the same species; we know that, but not all fleas know, and fleas sometimes transmit disease. The same goes for ticks.

Some human diseases can be transmitted by rabbits. These range from the common cold to the dread rabies. This is also true of pigeons, parakeets, dogs, cats, hamsters and every other living thing. Rabbits are no more or no less dangerous in this respect; all animal contacts should be made with thoughtfulness. Don't cough or sneeze at a rabbit any more than you would at another person.

Disabilities and Diseases

Prevention is easier, cheaper, more certain, more effective and more humane than cure of most rabbit ailments. So—practice hygiene on a regular basis; avoid crowding, furnish nutritious food and adequate fresh drinking water, eliminate vermin and flies, house your animals in clean dry quarters and protect them from molestation. It is really not difficult if you plan ahead and it is certainly no less than you would do for yourself. To put this aspect of rabbit keeping in perspective, a commercial establishment might lose 20% of its stock every year to disease. If you keep just a few animals under ideal conditions, you might lose one in twenty (5%) or at worst, one in ten (10%).

There are a few things not mentioned elsewhere in this book which you can do to improve your rabbit's quality of life. Let's review them here.

TOENAILS

Toenails—these are meant for digging and fighting. They grow constantly and they are normally sharp. When you visit a rabbitry, look at the person who handles the animals. You will likely see a heavy canvas apron or you will see a torn sweater. If your rabbits have especially long or twisted toenails, you should clip them. Use a tool available from your pet dealer or a diagonal pliers. Cut so as to stay well clear of the vein which extends into the base of each nail. You may have to trim nails every four months.

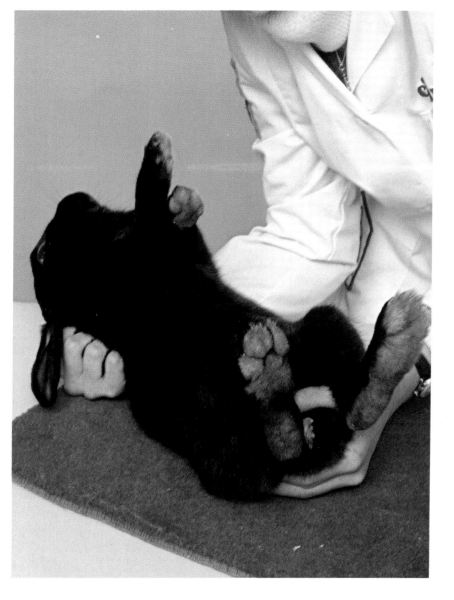

Opposite and above: Alycia examines a rabbit.
This is the way it should be done for a potential
purchase or a show. She works over a pad with a
non-slip surface, and she works close to the
animal, using both hands and forearms to cradle
and gently restrain it. Teeth, ears, vent, nails—all
get a careful and thorough examination.

TEETH

Teeth—the incisors, that is, grow continuously for the lifetime of the rabbit. They also wear down as the rabbit eats its food and gnaws at its cage. In some instances you might offer a boiled ham bone to a persistent gnawer. Rarely will the incisors grow out of control. Eventually, then the rabbit would starve. You can clip the teeth or have a veterinarian do it for you, but this is a most unusual situation.

SORE HOCKS AND BROKEN BACKS

You have heard of Thumper? Well, that's typical male rabbit behavior. They are generally mute animals but thumping serves to transmit signals. The trouble is, thumping was designed for the earth and not for a wire cage floor. Some rabbits end up with sore hocks from thumping or stamping, especially bucks. If a rabbit stamps hard enough it can even break its own back! If a predatory animal attempts to get into a rabbit cage, the rabbit might end up with a broken back although the predator may never have touched it.

Sore hocks also occur as a result of rough cage bottoms and infections associated with unsanitary conditions.

Sometimes, however, the problem is an inherited genetic defect. If you cannot get the injured part to heal after treatment with antiseptic you might be well advised to destroy the animal. Thin fur on the feet is a genetic trait which predisposes this disability.

VENEREAL DISEASE

Infectious venereal diseases are sometimes transmitted between rabbits when they mate. You may see small blisters, scabs or ulcers around the sex organs of bred rabbits. Penicillin is the drug to cure this disease. The dosage is 50,000 units per day for three days.

WET DEWLAPS

A wet dewlap is usually a disability, not necessarily a disease. You are the culprit since your watering system just doesn't fit your rabbit's drinking style. Clip away the wet matted hair and dust the affected area with cornstarch to dry it. Then re-arrange the water supply or raise the water crock to keep the rabbit from getting his neck wet.

WRY NECK

Infectious wry neck causes the animal to twist its head. One eye may roll up or back, and the rabbit may lose its balance and fall over when it tries to walk. The cause might well be an infestation of mites in the ears or it might be an infection of the ear or inner ear. Go after the mites with olive oil, mineral oil or a medicinal mite eliminator. Go after the infection with penicillin or, better still, tetracycline.

TAPEWORM

Tapeworm causes general poor health. There is no treatment, but what you must do is to get after the source of the trouble. The parasitic worm got to your rabbit from a dog or a cat directly or with the help of a mouse or a roach. If a dog with tapeworms simply sleeps on the hay you use for rabbit hutch bedding, your rabbits may become parasitized. The rabbit is an intermediate host—this means that the tapeworm eventually leaves the rabbit for his real goal in life, another dog or cat.

WARBLES

A warble is a swelling under the skin caused by the larvae of a bot fly. Remove it by lancing and tweezering out the maggot. Clean the wound with antiseptic and it should heal with no aftereffects.

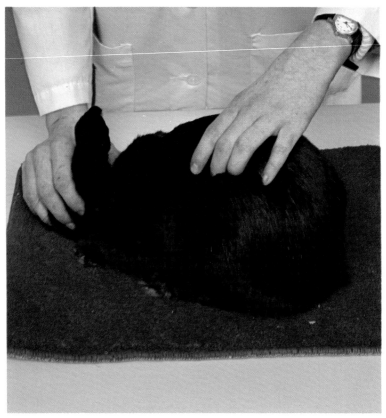

While the back is examined for over-all soundness, the head is gently but firmly held down.

Opposite:
Ears should be checked periodically for parasites and other problems.

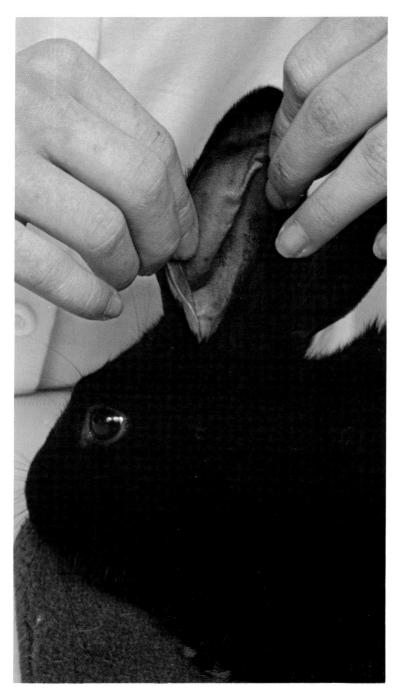

SNUFFLES

Snuffles is a common infectious disease. The symptoms are sneezing, matted fur on the front feet (caused by rubbing the runny nose), nasal discharge and inflamed eyes. The cause is crowding and poor housekeeping. The cure is to correct the cause and to treat affected animals with a broad spectrum antibiotic.

SLAUGHTERING

Millions of rabbits are killed for food every year quickly and effectively. The method is the same if you have just one old suffering pet or thousands going to market. It is described and illustrated in every book and pamphlet dealing with meat rabbits. Here is how it comes across from the U.S. Department of Agriculture's Handbook No. 309.

> The preferred method of slaughtering a rabbit is by dislocating the neck. Hold the animal by its hind legs with the left hand. Place the thumb of the right hand on the neck just back of the ears, with the four fingers extended under the chin. Push down on the neck with the right hand, stretching the animal. Press down with the thumb. Then raise the animal's head by a quick movement and dislocate the neck. The animal becomes unconscious and ceases struggling. This method is instantaneous and painless when done correctly.

This informative government publication goes on to describe the method of skinning and preparing the carcass for the cook. It is available at a reasonable price from the Superintendent of Documents, U.S. Government Printing Office, Washington, DC 20402.

Age is not a disease; call it a disability. An old rabbit becomes stiff, slow, senile, infertile, blind and subject to disease. A quick painless death is then an act of mercy.

Breeding

The young are born 28 to 35 days after a fertile doe and a buck mate. Virtually 99% of all litters arrive on the thirty-first day. Call them kittens or pups or bunnies. There might be as many as a dozen.

A female of a small variety will be ready to breed at six months, but the giant breeds mature more slowly; give them nine months. Males should be two months older than females before you begin to use them as breeders. Most experienced rabbit breeders tell us that once a doe is mature she should be bred promptly. If she is not bred until, say, 18 months or two years, it is possible that she may never produce any reasonable numbers of healthy, normal young.

When you mate rabbits, always bring the female to the cage of the male. Keep them together (if they don't fight) for a few hours. After they mate, the male may fall on his side and lie still for a little while. This is no guarantee that they mated, but it is a good sign. Also he may stamp or jerk his body or squeal; good, but still no guarantee.

If she has a litter a month after they mated, then you can be *sure*. The rest is pure guesswork.

The big bugaboo in rabbit breeding is "false pregnancy". Even the term "false pregnancy" is a bit sticky. It is possible for a fertile female to be mated and inseminated and for the ova to be fertilized and for the embryos to develop for a week or two. She is certainly pregnant. There is no such thing in nature as "slightly pregnant".

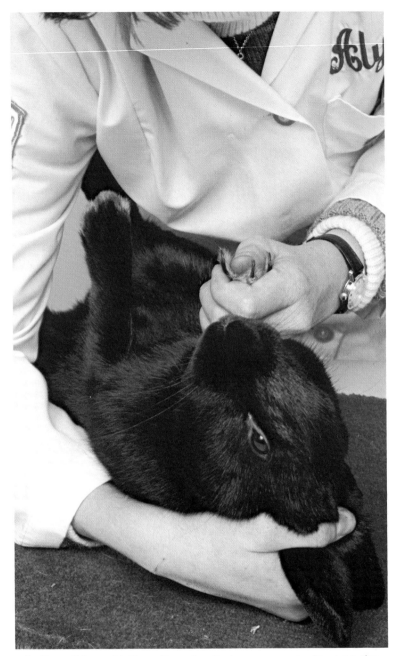

In the wild, a rabbit's nails naturally become worn down as the animal travels across different surfaces.

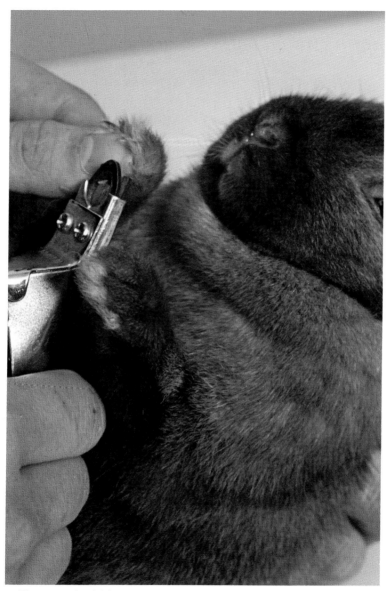

The caged rabbit must rely on its owner to clip its nails. Pet dealers can provide the proper tool for doing this maintenance job.

But if there is a shortage of food or she is harassed or molested, the embryos will stop developing and will be reabsorbed. This is not premature birth or abortion but rather that the female rabbit will reverse the process of pregnancy and her unborn babies will be absorbed within her placenta. Among rabbits under stress this happens all the time. It is nature's way of limiting the population with a minimum energy loss. It is also nature's way of generating a tremendous population explosion if a colony of rabbits suddenly comes onto a field of clover and simultaneously discovers that the only fox in the county was just run over by a motorcycle.

What must you do after your rabbits are mated?

1.) Separate them.

2.) Provide the female with a nest box containing some hay. The nest box for a four-pound rabbit might well be 1' x 2' x 10 inches high. You can build or you can buy nest boxes. They should be simple and strong.

Remember that your domestic rabbit descended from a wild creature that lived in a dark nest at the end of a long earthen tunnel. The most successful rabbit breeders leave their does strictly alone after they have been mated. Visitors, other animals, noise, tobacco smoke, flashing lights—these are all distractions which certainly cannot improve the productivity of your animals.

There are methods of palpating the abdomen of a female rabbit to determine if she is pregnant. Great! Do it every day and if she is pregnant she might just be so upset by your fooling around that she resorbs her entire litter.

If a pregnant female rabbit is properly cared for, she probably will pluck the hair from her belly to expose her teats. She has about eight. The hair she plucks will become a liner in the nest box with no help from you.

If on that thirty-first day she produces more babies than she has teats, what happens? Well, sometimes they all make it and sometimes the weak ones fade away; sometimes the rabbit keeper finds he has another female that gave birth within a day and that this female has a small litter. He resorts to fostering and sometimes he saves a few bunnies this way—no guarantee, but worth a try.

Leave the doe with her youngsters about six to eight weeks or until they are on solid food. Breed her again soon if you are in the meat business or wait a while if you want the best quality, best nourished progeny.

Keep one buck for every two or three or four or five does. Keep bucks apart from each other or one will surely be killed. Remember that wild rabbits can run away, but caged animals have nowhere to go but Heaven.

If you want to graduate to pedigreed registered purebred exhibition specimens, then you should join a rabbit breeder's society and plan to tattoo every animal. This need not be done until the baby rabbit is weaned.

Bear in mind that ever since Roman times, people have been figuring out new and better schemes for breeding rabbits. To start right you should start simple and use a system which has withstood the test of time. Mate a mature female to a mature male and then isolate her with plenty of fresh food, water, bedding and a nest box with hay in it. Leave her alone for 35 days unless it is obvious that she is not pregnant. Now, that is simple. After you have produced a few litters in your rabbitry you can begin to complicate the process, but you may well discover that simple is best.

Any male domestic rabbit may be mated with any female domestic rabbit and living fertile young will be born, but it is not wise to breed mongrels. If you have a Flemish or a Lop or a Dutch or an Angora, you should mate it to another of the same variety. Some rabbit varieties took a hundred or more years to perfect; a reason for breaking the chain would have to be very compelling.

Alycia holds down one rabbit with her forearm while she examines another. This is a tricky procedure, but she knows exactly what she is doing.

Opposite:
A rabbit will often remain still if it has been placed and held in this manner (above) for a few seconds. While the animal is still, it is marked with a tattoo for life-long identification (below), a must for any rabbit which is exhibited.

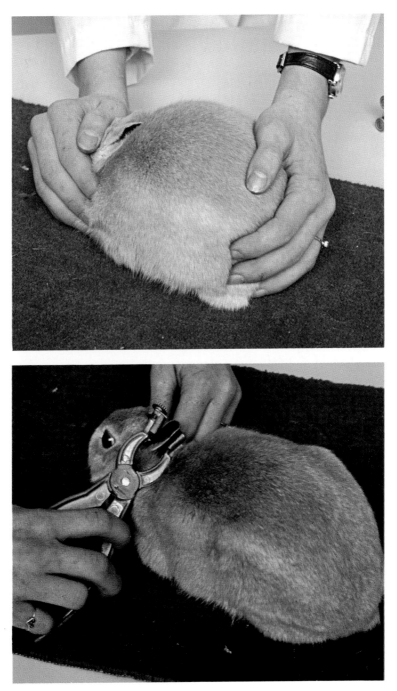

Rabbit Timetable

Kindled—Blind, hairless, average weight two ounces		First day
Eyes open		10th day
Begin to eat solid food		21st day
Weaned	Normal	56th day
	Minimum	28th day
Puberty	New Zealand Male	5 - 6 months
	New Zealand Female	4 - 5 months
	Dutch Male	4 - 5 months
	Dutch Female	3 - 4 months
Breeding age	New Zealand Male & Female	5½ - 6½ months
	Dutch Male & Female	4½ - 5½ months
Gestation period	Normal	31 days
	Extremes	29 - 35 days
Reproductive period	average	2.5 years
Lifetime	average	5 years
	Maximum	13 years

Rabbit fertility in caged animals is just about a 12 month thing, but if you really watch closely and keep records of large numbers, you may find that your animals are more productive in late winter and spring as the days grow longer. It is not necessary to avoid breeding rabbits any time during the year unless you keep them outdoors in parts of the country where the climate is really extremely hot in summer or fiercely cold in winter. Of course in those instances you will have to provide ventilation or special insulated housing to protect them.

It would be neat and tidy to be able to report that the bigger a rabbit is, the bigger its litter is, but this is not entirely true. Yes, dwarfs such as the Netherland Dwarf and the Polish usually produce no more than four young at a time, but the New Zealand and the Californian (which are not the largest) can be expected to give birth to as many as ten at a time. The really giant breeds don't do much more than that. For example, a senior Flemish Giant doe might weigh nearly twice as much as a junior Californian, but her litters will average about the same. Thank Mother Nature for this, since the normal number of teats on any doe is only eight.

If you want maximum production you can schedule a breeding program to get four litters per year from each good doe. The youngsters should remain with their dam until they are weaned and eating solid food—what you feed your animals will help determine how fast they develop. It will take surely six weeks and possibly eight weeks to wean a normal litter. Don't push.

To end this chapter on breeding, you should bear in mind that good does will fizzle out as breeders after about two years of production. Really superior does might last three years. Once in a while you might even encounter a doe that is still at it in her sixth year, but that would be one for the record books. Bucks might last a little longer. And then, that's the end.

The show secretary is the first person an exhibitor meets. A small fee is usually collected, space is assigned and coded numbers for identifying the animals are recorded.

Opposite:
As the judge examines a rabbit, he will comment to his secretary. If there are a dozen entries in a class, it would be impossible (and unfair) to expect the judge to remember every virtue and every fault of each animal.

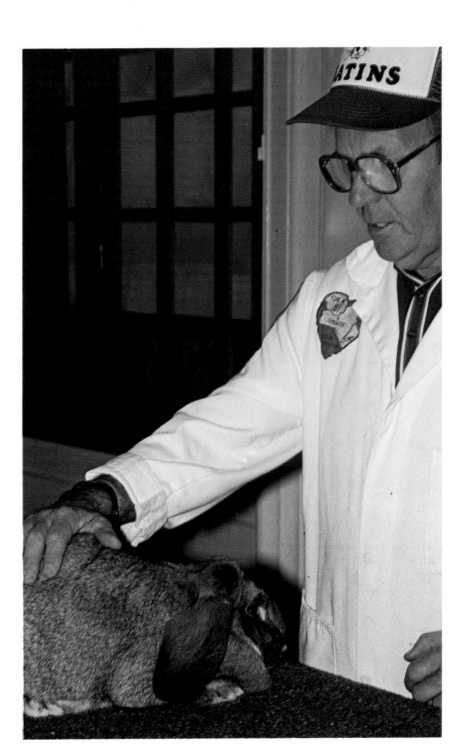

Genetics is an exact and complicated science, but anyone can master a few of its basic principles.

Genetics

No two living organisms which were produced sexually are absolutely identical. They vary. To get an identical copy, one must resort to non-sexual methods such as grafting or cloning.

We encounter variation. It is a natural fact of life. What we do with variation is called selective breeding and how we do it is by applying what we know about genetics. One might say that genetics is the code. As we decipher it, we learn how to manipulate the variables and to the extent that we did it right, we have rabbits with patterns, colors, hair length, hair texture, size, ear form and body shape as we anticipated. We also have (when we do it wrong) troubles with infertility, small litters, nervousness, sore hocks, poor stamina and bad dispositions.

You don't need a college degree in zoology or mastery of a computer or a lot of money to successfully improve a species of domestic animal by application of genetic principles. What you do need is a lot of patience and a little information to get you started. Remember that it took centuries of selective breeding to give us the varieties we have today; consider that you are doing a good job if you are able to maintain what we presently have. A slight improvement in any strain would be a great job and a really new established and worthwhile variety would entitle you to a notation on your tombstone.

This is an attempt to demonstrate what can be done to

This is a Dutch-marked rabbit. The Dutch pattern can be bred into many rabbit varieties and can be established in many colors. It is also possible to establish this pattern in mice, rats and cavies, but in no way are these similarly marked species otherwise related.

rabbit colors and patterns without explaining all about how genetics works. If you are bitten by the bug, there are plenty of good books to explain the process in detail. Here let's just see what happens in a few instances.

Mate two albinos of the same strain. They will produce only albinos. This is because since the albino gene is recessive, both parents must be pure albino to look that way. There is no other latent genetic material in an albino to cause color. How about the two albinos which when mated produced some colored young? Yes, this is theoretically possible if the parents were albinos by virtue of non-matching chromosomes. You can accept that little gem on faith or you can study genetics in a more formal and systematic way.

To move forward, you should understand that the genes are the building blocks and that for each characteristic of an animal, there are two matched groups of genes at work. One comes from each parent. Some genes represent dominant traits such as agouti color. We tabulate these traits with abbreviations and as a convention, the dominant trait (agouti, for example) is given a capital letter *A* and the recessive is shown in lower case *a*.

When a dominant trait was inherited, this is usually what you get to *see*. If a pure agouti rabbit *AA* was mated to a self colored rabbit *aa*, the offspring would all *look* agouti, but they would carry a hidden recessive gene for self color which a skilled breeder might be able to re-establish by applying certain known facts.

Here are the diagrams that show what happens. Take it slowly. Read it a few times if necessary. It's like riding a bicycle—after a while it will be easy.

Two pure agouti (*AA*)

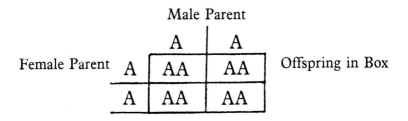

	Male Parent		
	A	A	
A	AA	AA	Offspring in Box
A	AA	AA	

Female Parent shown at left.

All 100% of the offspring will be pure agouti.

Now let's take a pure agouti rabbit (*AA*) and mate it to a self rabbit (*aa*).

	A	A
a	Aa	Aa
a	Aa	Aa

83

One hundred per cent of the offspring will *look like* their agouti parent. The *A* is dominant over the *a* and it determines what the animal *looks like*. The *a* is recessive and is hidden in the genetic make-up of the animal. If you have agoutis with this recessive trait, you can re-establish a strain of selfs (*aa*) by selective breeding and application of established genetic principles.

Try mating two heterozygous (there is a new word for you) agouti-self rabbits. Call the buck *Aa* and the doe *Aa*, also. Heterozygous means that the genes *A* and *a* are not identical.

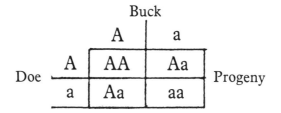

The long haul statistical prediction for this mating is
        one *AA*
        two *Aa*
        one *aa*

Therefore, *statistically speaking,*
    1. 25% will be (*AA*), pure agouti
    2. 50% will be (*Aa*), heterozygous (there is that new word that sneaked in) and
    3. 25% will be (*aa*) pure self rabbits.

Note that this is a *statistical probability* of what will happen. If the doe kindles just one offspring it could be *AA* or *Aa* or *aa*. Also, just by the luck of the draw, she might produce seven self babies.

If you pair up two selfs the result is predictable, and it looks like this:

	a	a
a	aa	aa
a	aa	aa

100% of the offspring will be *aa* self. Call the parents and their offspring homozygous for self because the genes we are interested in (for self color) are all the same. Even if there is but one baby rabbit, it is going to be a self colored specimen. The word homozygous means that the genes *a* and *a* are identical.

One could create a chart for every known genetic trait of every organism. It would fill volumes. For the moment at least, don't bother, but just to demonstrate what we have to work with, here is a list of just *some* of the *more common* genetic traits of rabbits which *have been* studied and charted. Remember that a capital letter designates a dominant trait and a lower case letter is used for a recessive trait. Also remember that these various traits are grouped here as they are linked in nature. For example, there is no connection between self color and blue eyes, since those genes don't seem to interact, but agouti, tan and self are linked.

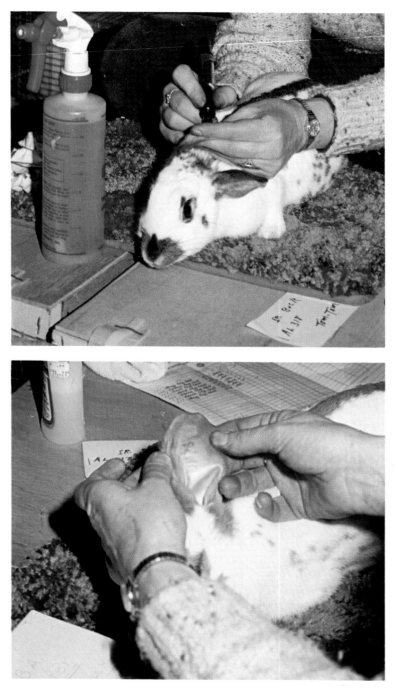

The judge examines the identifying number in the ear of the rabbit.

Opposite:
Since the judge must not know who owns a rabbit, the animal's ear is marked with a coded number assigned by the show secretary (above). While an ear tattoo is permanent, the number assigned by the show secretary may be washed off after the prizes are awarded (below).

Listing of common genetic traits of rabbits. (Capital letters indicate dominant traits; lower case letters indicate recessive traits.)

Genetic Trait	Symbol
Agouti	A
Tan	At
Self	a
Black	B
Brown	b
Color	C
Dark Chinchilla	cchd
Medium Chinchilla	cchm
Light Chinchilla	cchl
Himalayan	ch
Albino	c
Color Density	D
Dilute color	d
Blackness	Ed
As in Agouti	E
As in Harlequin	ej
As in yellows and tortoise	e
Vienna White	V
Blue-eyed white	v
Spotted	En
Not spotted	en
Dutch	
Dutch Patterned	du
Dutch Patterned variant	duw
Dutch Patterned second variant	dud
Wide Band	
Normal Agouti	W
Yellow band wider than normal	w

Rex
   Rex coat   r
   German Short-haired rex r_2
   Normandy rex r_3
   Normal   R

Angora
   Long hair   l
   Normal   L

Satin
   Satin coat   sa
   Normal coat   Sa

Wavy coat
   Waved coat   wa
   Normal coat   Wa

This is but a smattering. There is nothing here about ears or dewlaps or size and very little about eye color. Additionally, there are genes that modify others and cause shading of colors.

Let's try another application of genetic principles, this time to establish albinos when you have only one.

For example: you have an albino doe *cc* and you want to breed albinos but your best senior buck is a New Zealand red *CC*. Go ahead, breed them. Then seven months later breed the best buck of the litter *Cc* back to his mother. We will assume that the senior buck is pure (homozygous) for red. That is why we designate him *CC*. The doe is albino. Since albino is recessive, she is surely pure (homozygous) albino. That is why we are certain when we designate her *cc*. The progeny of that mating of

The judge gently raises the head of this Netherland Dwarf while with the other hand he keeps it from backing away.

Opposite:
Mr. A. Burke, the judge, is checking claws. In the course of one day, he will have looked at thousands; it's hard work.

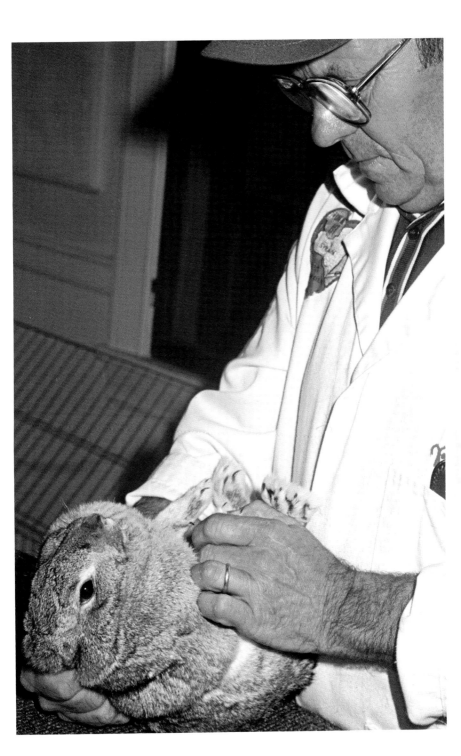

CC x *cc* will be 100% *Cc* regardless of their sex. Follow this selective breeding program with charts.

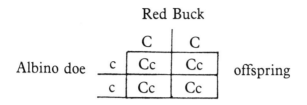

All the offspring will be red because of the dominant gene *C*, but each will carry a recessive gene for albino *c*. Call them *Cc*, heterozygous.

Mate a young buck *Cc* to his mother *cc*.

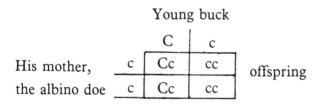

We can expect that 50% of the offspring will be colored and 50% will be albino. So now you have a good chance to keep going with albinos even though you didn't have a pair of albino rabbits in the beginning. Of course this took two generations and at least six months elapsed, but that's how it is done and that's why it took a thousand or so years to get where we are today.

Earlier in this chapter you saw a prediction for the outcome of a mating and the remark that it was a "statistical probability." If that confused you, look at it another way. Consider people and their sex. Over the long haul we can predict that about half of the new population will be boys and the other half will be girls. The reason is linked to the mechanics of our genes.

Now look at families you know, families with two, three, four or even five girls in a row! Or as many boys in a row. It happens. It is much the same as rolling dice. Even though the odds for human sex are 50/50, it is possible to run up a considerable number of one without enountering the other. Briefly, then, unless the prediction is for 100% of a particular trait or pattern or color, you should not expect each and every litter to come forth in precisely the ratio developed from a chart. If you look at, say, 100 rabbits which were bred to prove out a simple, uncomplicated genetic trait, you would find that the predictions do come true.

If you were breeding pigeons or parrots or certain species of tropical fishes, you would want equal numbers of both sexes since it takes one parent of each sex to raise the young. Not so with rabbits. One buck will need only to make momentary visits to satisfy the requirements of several does. A second buck could easily destroy all domestic tranquility. What if your first doe presents you with a litter of five little bucks and no does?

How often might this happen? What are the odds? Every rabbit breeder, and every other gambler who wonders about probabilities, should doff his hat to Blaise Pascal. This philosopher, physicist, mathematician, genius was born in France on the 19th of June 1623. His family was ennobled by King Louis XI in 1478, but they elected not to affix the honorary "de" to their name.

Blaise Pascal contributed to our understanding of air pressure and performed pioneering experiments with a mercury barometer. He solved mathematical problems involving cycloids and optical projection. He developed

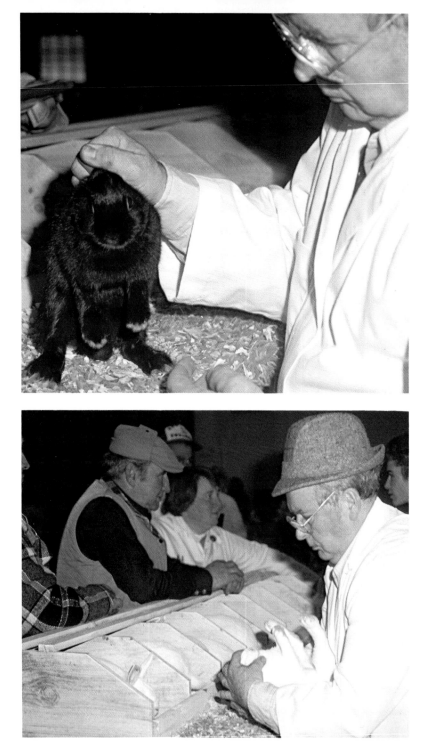

This Dwarf is being lined up for judging. Rabbits generally sit quite still during this procedure.

Opposite:
The judge gently lifts the rabbit (above) by grasping the loose skin over its shoulders. The judging table (below) is tended by volunteers who move the rabbits to and from their cages. The judge, Mr. L. McGuire, doesn't know who owns the rabbit he is examining. He refers to it only by number. His secretary records his comments for every animal.

Pascal's *Triangle of Odds*

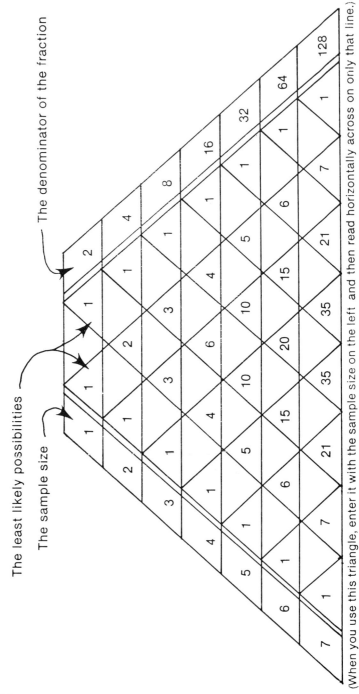

The denominator of the fraction

The least likely possibilities

The sample size

(When you use this triangle, enter it with the sample size on the left and then read horizontally across on only that line.)

96

concepts to show the difference between knowledge and belief, between reason and opinion; he was comfortable with both. Sadly for mankind, he lived only 39 years.

For rabbit breeders and other gamblers, he invented a table of odds. It requires no knowledge of mathematics to use it. The table is known as Pascal's Triangle and it is probably the simplest thing he ever did. Notice that each of the numbers (more than one) was obtained by adding the two nearest numbers in the line above. This tells us that the base can be extended downward as far as we care to carry it. For any computation of odds, all the information appears *on just one line.* Choose a random sample of any reasonable size. A litter of five rabbits is a reasonable size. Look at the fifth line of Pascal's Triangle; 1 - 5- 10 - 10 - 5 - 1. Add these numbers. They total 32. That total (32) becomes the denominator in all the fractions that follow. Now you can do some predicting. Consider first a least likely possibility and Pascal will give you the odds. Do you remember the famous entertainer Eddie Cantor? He was the father of a number of daughters and no sons. Pascal's lines tell us the odds for least likely possibilities with any number of offspring. That of course would be for them to all be the same sex. Let's say the number of offspring is five. The odds here are one in thirty-two. For one to be of the opposite sex, the odds drop to five in thirty-two. For two out of five to be one sex and the other three to be the opposite sex the chances are ten in thirty-two and the same goes for the sexes reversed.

As an aside, it should be noted that when it comes to sex, people and rabbits and other creatures too are not as rigidly fixed as we lead ourselves to believe. The ratio of sexes in rabbits is higher for males, more nearly 53:47 than 50:50. In humans too it is slightly tilted, but for our purposes 50:50 is close enough.

It doesn't matter whether all the offspring were born simultaneously or over the course of years. Any random

Above and opposite: Angora rabbits should be groomed several hours a week. Don't keep Angoras unless you can devote a lot of time to their hair care.

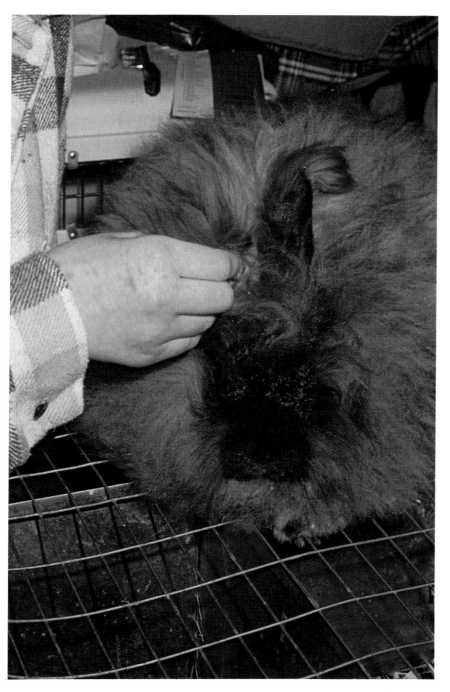

sample is valid. Sex is not the only variable you can figure odds on.

Pascal's Triangle is applicable to any simple yes - no situation. Typical are the simple heterozygous-dominant x homozygous-recessive crosses we previously looked at. *Aa* x *aa* or *Cc* x *cc* crosses are in this category.

Heterozygous

		A	a
Homozygous	a	Aa	aa
	a	Aa	aa

The expectancy is still 50:50, but the probability (odds) of getting what we expect depends on how many individuals we have to work with. If we apply the formula to this breeding scheme because we were trying to establish a pure recessive strain of *aa* or *cc* or whatever, we would see that in a litter of four there would be one chance in sixteen that none of the offspring would be the desired variety. In a litter of five the possibility of total failure would be less, only one in thirty-two and in a litter of six, one chance in sixty-four that there still would be none of what you really wanted. That's a lot of rabbits.

Try out Pascal's Triangle with this example: You want a pair but are unable to recognize the sexes in a litter of baby rabbits. What are the odds for getting a pair if you pick five at random? Enter the triangle on the left at 5 and read across to 32. A least likely possibility would be to have all five of one sex. The odds for this are one in thirty-two. The other least likely possibility would be all five of the other sex. The odds for this are also 1 in 32. So then there are two in thirty-two chances of getting all males or all females. Each of the other thirty out of thirty-two possibilities will provide both sexes; so the odds are 30/32 or nearly 94%; the house takes nothing.

100

Economics

If you want to make money from meat, raise sheep or swine or cattle or poultry. The only way a rabbit can compete is if there is a combination of special markets, inexpensive food supplies, cheap land and cheap labor. For example, a Peace Corps volunteer in Ghana (formerly Gold Coast) was able to make rabbit raising worthwhile because most of these criteria for success were met. By contrast, after Australia and New Zealand were firmly settled and established, the first thing the people did was to try to control all those millions of rabbits. Why?

Well, one reason is that rabbits are very choosy about their diet—they will wipe out all their favorite foods and soon only the coarse and bitter plants will remain to dominate the landscape. By contrast, sheep and goats will clean up the briars and "weeds" and with a little management they actually improve their pastures.

A second reason why rabbits are not competitive with sheep or cattle or pigs is found in their long-term productivity. When the animals are in equilibrium with their pasture—neither cropping it to death nor letting it go to seed—it will be found that there is produced more mutton or beef or pork per acre than rabbit meat. Of course, every rabbit generates not only its meat but also its fur. Unfortunately, rabbit fur is not especially valuable. When a mink or a fox brings fifty dollars you would be lucky to get fifty cents for a properly dried rabbit skin.

Angora wool is also great for gloves and sweaters and novelties, but if you start with a ton of alfalfa and oats you will get more wool from Shropshire sheep than from Angora rabbits.

A large rabbit (opposite) could be dangerous if it were not tame. Don't ever handle a rabbit unles you (1) know the animal and (2) know exactly how to go about it. This method of lifting a *small* rabbit (right) is all right so long as you are able to grasp it firmly without undue squeezing. This old Lop (below) is so tame and experienced that it would stand still on a cigar box for an hour, but it is still a good precaution to keep a hand on it.

Without belaboring the point; it is an economic fact of life that even though the rabbit is explosively prolific, it cannot compete with the larger domestic herbivores unless there is some combination of special circumstances. One such special circumstance is in the city or the suburbs. Zoning and health laws and small house lots make it impossible to keep cattle, swine or even sheep. Chickens can be noisy, but rabbits are frequently just the ticket.

Cages are easy to build and do not take too much room or cost too much money; and the basic diet can be supplemented by making arrangements with a baker for stale bread and with a grocer for vegetable tops and clippings.

Your best start would be to start small for fun; then you lose nothing if there is no profit. The world is full of people who were suckered into the rabbit business because they read advertisements such as these: "Fantastic Profits from Rabbits", "Rabbits that Earn for You" or "Make Money with Rabbits". Forget it. Pull in your horns, stop dreaming, be practical. If your local pet shop can use 50 or more a year, especially around Easter, this is great and if a local butcher wants a few hundred a year, that's great too, but you ought to sit down with a pencil and calculate what those twenty or more cages and the food will cost. Remember too that one or two cages might fit in the garage or basement, but how about two dozen cages that must be equipped with food and water and kept clean 365 days per year? There is also a genuine market in rabbits for research, but this is not for a beginner. Those animals must be pedigreed stock, bred, fed and cared for under the strictest control. This is a field which only an experienced breeder can enter with any chance for success.

Start right with rabbits, start for fun and then if things go well, then and only then *perhaps* you can make a business out of it.

Rabbit Talk

Here are a few words you will hear and may get to use as you work with your animals and meet others who do the same.

KINDS OF RABBITS

Breed - A kind of rabbit which consistently reproduces rabbits like itself. This could be, for example, the New Zealand breed or the Californian breed.

Dwarf - A rabbit which, when mature, weighs no more than three pounds.

Medium - A rabbit which, when mature, weighs no more than nine to twelve pounds.

Giant - A rabbit which, when mature, weighs more than twelve pounds.

Strain - A family of rabbits which exhibits the same genetic characteristics.

Line - A strain.

Variety - A particular color within a breed, that is, red or albino or some other thing that makes it different.

Type - Conformation of body, like cobby or racy.

Cobby - Short, stocky. A Florida White is cobby; so is an English Lop.

Racy - Slim, slender. A Belgian Hare is racy; so is a Himalayan.

Charlie - A rabbit whose color pattern is more lightly marked than normal.

Marked rabbits, such as Dutch-marked littermates (opposite), are rarely identical, even in the same litter. This Dutch-marked show specimen (right) is also a good pet—there is no reason why a pet cannot be shown. The Dutch-marked, albino and English Spot (below) all eat the same food, have the same habits and require the same care.

BREEDERS JARGON

Breeder - A person who breeds rabbits and also a rabbit which is used for breeding.

Buck - A male rabbit.

Doe - A female rabbit.

False Pregnancy - When *you* think a doe should kindle, but she doesn't.

Gestation - Those 31 days more or less between breeding and kindling.

Kindling - Giving birth.

Linebreeding - Successive generations of inbreeding to preserve certain qualities. A buck might be mated to his daughter and then to his granddaughter.

Pair - A male and a female which have been mated.

Purebred - A member of an established and recognized breed.

Test-mating - Accomplished by bringing the doe back to the buck about eight days after the mating. If she rejects his advances, it is probable that she is pregnant.

Palpation - Feeling the abdomen of a bred doe to determine if she is pregnant. A beginner is well advised to just wait and see.

AGES OF A RABBIT

Kitten, Bunny, Pup - All names for a rabbit which is not yet weaned.

Junior - A rabbit under the age of six months.

Senior - A mature rabbit. Smaller rabbits mature in six months and those over ten pounds at maturity are classed as Seniors when they reach eight months.

RABBIT HAIR

Angora - The coat grows to a length of at least three inches; color is immaterial. If the hair is three inches long, it is an Angora.

These Dutch-marked rabbits (right) are only eleven days old. Palpating a doe to determine whether or not she is pregnant (below) is better left to the experienced breeder.

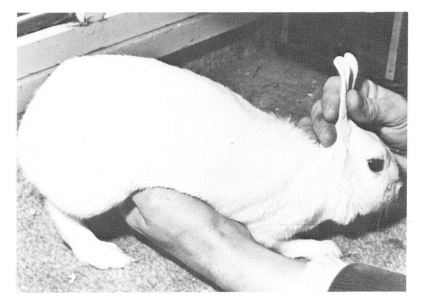

Compare the ears of a "normal" rabbit with those of a Dwarf and a Lop. These varieties represent a great deal of effort and should not be crossbred.

Opposite:
The breed of rabbit known as the Chinchilla (above) is still a rabbit and not a rodent, but it is called a Chinchilla because of its fur. The ring pattern of the fur can be seen by gently blowing a stream of air at the rump of the animal (below). Regardless of the color, this pattern is derived from the wild agouti pelt.

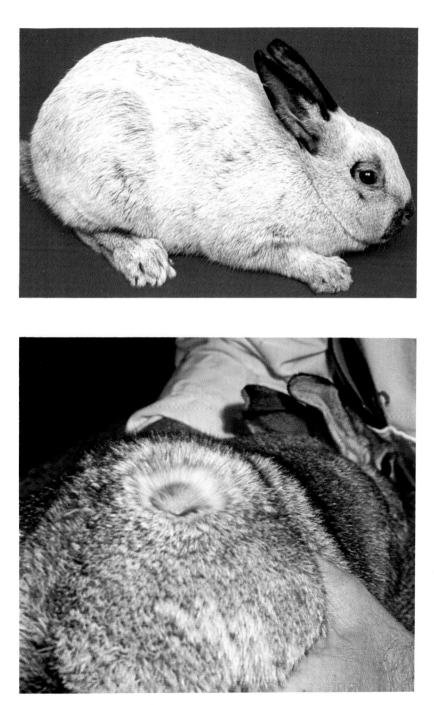

111

Quite a bit of hair can be pulled from an Angora rabbit, but *many* piles of hair the size of this one would be needed to make a sweater.

Density - Relative thickness of the coat of fur.

Guard Hair - Coarse long hair.

Under fur - Shorter soft hair.

Flyback - Fur that quickly returns to its normal arrangement after it is brushed or blown the wrong way.

Molt - Shedding of fur.

Rex - Short-haired rabbit; hair like plush.

Satin - Hair is partly transparent and lustrous.

Ticking - The effect caused by long guard hairs contrasting with the color of the body fur called under-wool. Typical of this effect is to be seen in the Belgian Hare and the Flemish Giant.

Odd Facts about Rabbits

Mentioned elsewhere in this book is the perfectly normal process of coprophagy, also called pseudorumination. Some other animals are known to eat fecal matter, but the exact method used by the rabbit is not known elsewhere in the animal kingdom.

Several more odd things about rabbits are to be noted in their reproduction. For one thing, the ova (eggs) of the rabbit are among the largest of any mammal. Rabbit eggs are reported to be 160 microns in diameter. Since a micron is 1/1000 of a millimeter, we have an egg 160/1000mm or 0.160mm. This is not very large in absolute terms, but you can see individual eggs during autopsy without any magnifying device. Compared to an ostrich egg, it really is insignificant, but compared to eggs of other mammals, it is large. For example, a human ovum (egg) is 0.136mm and bear in mind that the rabbit egg at 0.160mm came from an animal which weighs only one-twentieth of the weight of a human. Graphically speaking, a rabbit egg is about as large as the period printed at the end of this sentence, and a human egg is a trifle smaller than that.

Also as noted elsewhere is the ability of the doe to resorb her embryos if conditions are not right. This is a most efficient response to an adverse environmental change such as stress or lack of food or bad weather or whatever.

Still another odd fact about rabbits is that the female

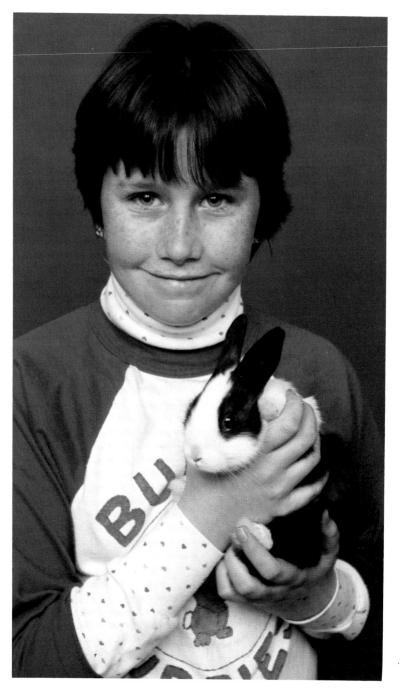

A white Angora is shown here with a long-haired cavy, also known as a guinea pig. Angora skins and wool are desirable, but there is no commercial use for cavy fur or pelts.

Opposite:
This Dutch-marked Dwarf is nearly full grown but hardly larger than a cavy.

does not have sharply defined scheduled periods when she is receptive to the advances of the male. Instead, if she is not nursing her young or already pregnant or in a state of pseudo-pregnancy which might last 16 or so days, she will permit copulation and subsequently ovulate and become pregnant. In the rabbit, ovulation follows mating. In most other mammals the process is reversed.

Rabbits have been born to does who were never inseminated. That is, no male rabbit semen ever entered the doe and yet she generated embryos which developed. This phenomenon is common in some insects and even known in one species of lizard, producing a race of females; turkeys too have been produced this way, but among mammals it is highly unusual. A parthenogenetically produced rabbit is always a female and is for all intents and purposes merely a laboratory curiosity.

Some rabbits have gall bladders and they are normal. Some rabbits do not, but they seem to be perfectly normal too.

The earliest record of a white rabbit is a painting by Titian entitled *Madonna with Rabbit.* It was painted around 1550. It is very unlikely that Titian dreamed up a white rabbit.

If you believe in evil spirits you might want to ward them off by hanging the left hind foot of a rabbit around your neck on the midnight of a full moon. If you believe in good luck, you might want to get it by carrying a rabbit's foot in your pocket. If you believe what the Romans believed, you will feed rabbit meat to women as a beauty aid. If you believe in miracles and you want to get rich quick, get rid of your rabbits and buy lottery tickets; no one ever got rich quick on rabbits.

Males tend to be a trifle smaller than females of the same variety. Rabbits are born in a ratio of 53 males to 47 females.

A New Zealand doe and the progeny she produced in one twelve-month period.

Finally, in the list of odd facts is the very odd fact that a rabbit can be hypnotized. You can actually put a rabbit into a trance with typical deep breathing, fixed stare and partially closed eyes. A rabbit in such a trance can be injected with medicines, examined for injuries and otherwise gently handled. To hypnotize a rabbit, you should be alone with it in a quiet place. The rabbit should be supported belly-up between pillows. You should stroke the abdomen and chest gently in the direction the hair lies and also gently rub the sides and top of the head, pressing only slightly. Hum a little in a low monotone or talk quietly—this seems to help. Your subject will waken to a sudden noise or if it is moved from its inverted position.

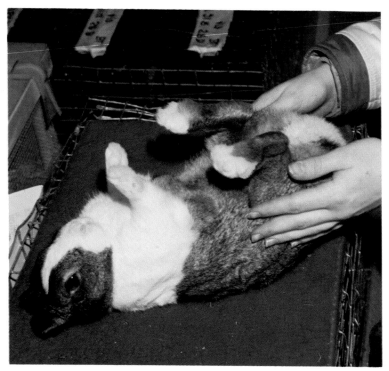

This is the first stage in hypnotizing a rabbit. Place it on its back and slowly stroke its sides.

Opposite:
The second step in hypnotizing a rabbit consists of gently stroking its abdomen (above). Sometimes it doesn't work. If its eyes "glaze," you did it. Once a rabbit is in a hypnotic trance (below), it will probably remain that way for several minutes unless disturbed. The sound of a handclap will break the trance.

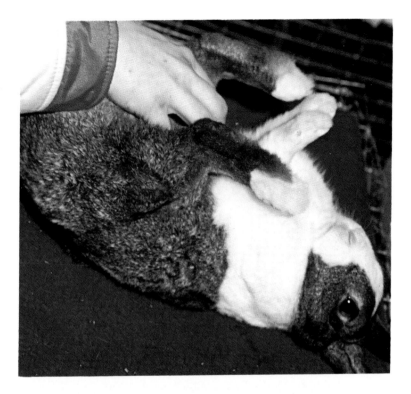

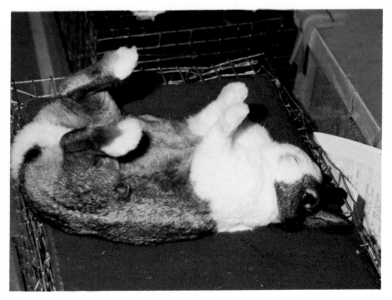

Dutch-marked rabbits are judged mainly on how sharply their pattern is defined.

Join the Club

If you would like to learn more about rabbits, join a club. If you want to share what you have already learned, join a club. If you want to improve your line or see how good rabbits can be, join a club. If you want to meet interesting people who share your enthusiasm for rabbits, join a club!

Most clubs are affiliated with a national organization which establishes standards and sanctions exhibitions and shows. In the U.S.A. today many thousands of fanciers belong to the American Rabbit Breeders Association (ARBA). They publish a magazine *Domestic Rabbits* bi-monthly and they invite your membership. Write: American Rabbit Breeders Asociation, 1925B South Main Street, Bloomington, IL 61701.

The British counterpart of the ARBA is the British Rabbit Council (BRC). They publish *Fur and Feather* 26 times a year and invite membership worldwide. Write to them: British Rabbit Council, Purfoy House, 7 Kirkgate, Newark, Nottingham, England.

Through these organizations you can reach local rabbit clubs and other people who are interested in these animals.

If you have doubts about conformation of a rabbit, hold it up against one which has already been awarded a prize in a competitive show.

Opposite:
This champion Angora won first prize in 1982 in Kingston, Massachusetts.

TRI-COUNTY
R. B. A.

KINGSTON
MASS.

FIRST
PLACE

123

INDEX

(Page numbers set in *italic* type refer to illustrations)